1,000,000 Books
are available to read at

Forgotten Books

www.ForgottenBooks.com

Read online
Download PDF
Purchase in print

ISBN 978-1-331-23004-5
PIBN 10161487

This book is a reproduction of an important historical work. Forgotten Books uses
state-of-the-art technology to digitally reconstruct the work, preserving the original format
whilst repairing imperfections present in the aged copy. In rare cases, an imperfection in
the original, such as a blemish or missing page, may be replicated in our edition. We do,
however, repair the vast majority of imperfections successfully; any imperfections that
remain are intentionally left to preserve the state of such historical works.

Forgotten Books is a registered trademark of FB &c Ltd.
Copyright © 2018 FB &c Ltd.
FB &c Ltd, Dalton House, 60 Windsor Avenue, London, SW19 2RR.
Company number 08720141. Registered in England and Wales.

For support please visit www.forgottenbooks.com

1 MONTH OF FREE READING

at
www.ForgottenBooks.com

By purchasing this book you are eligible for one month membership to ForgottenBooks.com, giving you unlimited access to our entire collection of over 1,000,000 titles via our web site and mobile apps.

To claim your free month visit: www.forgottenbooks.com/free161487

* Offer is valid for 45 days from date of purchase. Terms and conditions apply.

English
Français
Deutsche
Italiano
Español
Português

www.forgottenbooks.com

Mythology Photography **Fiction** Fishing Christianity **Art** Cooking Essays Buddhism Freemasonry Medicine **Biology** Music **Ancient Egypt** Evolution Carpentry Physics Dance Geology **Mathematics** Fitness Shakespeare **Folklore** Yoga Marketing **Confidence** Immortality Biographies Poetry **Psychology** Witchcraft Electronics Chemistry History **Law** Accounting **Philosophy** Anthropology Alchemy Drama Quantum Mechanics Atheism Sexual Health **Ancient History** **Entrepreneurship** Languages Sport Paleontology Needlework Islam **Metaphysics** Investment Archaeology Parenting Statistics Criminology **Motivational**

VISION

By FRANK CRANE

THE DAVIS PRESS,
WORCESTER, MASS.
MCMVI

COPYRIGHT, 1906
BY THE DAVIS PRESS,
WORCESTER, MASS.

(Most of these verses have appeared in the magazines, The Independent, The Century, Munsey's, The Youth's Companion; others are here printed for the first time.)

CONTENTS

Prelude
Vision
My Friends Remaining
Mater Matuta
Who Plants a Tree
The Sacrament of Spring
"I Am"
Live Like a Flower
Easter Greeting
Shepherd's Rest
The Little White Birches of New England
Three Things
The Lost Dream
Ballad of the Dead
My Friend
When She Comes Home
Christmas Wishes
The Gates of Heaven
The Loneliest Spot
The Answer

Truth
Morning on Lake Michigan
Why I Love You
The Little Green Snake
The Unchosen Cross
A Prayer
The Lost Word
Invitation to Vespers
The Waters of Bethlehem
The Three Ages
Rain on the Lake
8ale
Secret Woe
The Temple of Unbelief
Despair
"There is a Dimple"
"This, too, shall Pass"
Good-bye!
Sacred Heart
The Christ Child

To her who companies my life,
As perfect music makes poor words worth while,
I dedicate this, - - to my wife.

PRELUDE.

I have sung as the winds blow,
Speaking the random moods of a soul,
And of a soul familiar with great extremes,
Expressing black doubt as frankly as worship,
Now telling of bitterness, now of love,
Now of the outer glory of God's world,
Now of the inner mystery of the heart.
I have no Aim nor Purpose,
But have sung as the birds sing,
As children laugh or cry.
I never could make Pegasus plow.
What is written in this book
Is all as inconsistent as life is.
As for me, I am neither so good
Nor so bad as what I have written;
For one sings of the heights above him
And of the deeps below him,
And he knows both better than himself.

VISION.

Give me not scenes more charming; give me eyes
To see the beauty that around me lies;
To read the trail of souls, see angels shy
Among the faces of the passers-by.
I do not ask for sweeter music than
The common, daily Symphony of Man,
Could I but grasp its counterpoint, and see
How each discord melts toward harmony.

I do not ask for more to seek and love me,
I do not ask for brighter eyes to move me,
But sharper sense, to miss no hailing sign
Of fellowship in spirit seeking mine.
No golden shore I seek, but a heart that sings
The exquisite delight of common things.
The Kingdom of Heaven is not There, but Here—
O for the seeing eye and hearing ear!

MY FRIENDS REMAINING.

Lord, I do thank Thee for my friends,
   The few and true remaining:
Through falling years their love appears
   A rainbow through the raining.

I thank Thee for the bitter shame
   The false and weak brought o'er me;
For when through loss I found my Cross
   I saw One there before me.

And so I make Thee for my friends
   A genuine Thanksgiving;
And pray that those who seem my foes
   Scourge me to better living!

MATER MATUTA.

O day dawn, O gray dawn,
    Why are you standing there,
So still, so still, behind the trees,
    With your arms outstretched in prayer?

O day dawn, O pale dawn,
    Why is your face distressed?
Have you, too, had a little child
    To die upon your breast?

O day dawn, O cool dawn,
    Touching my fevered head,
At my window I've waited all night for you,
    Watching beside my dead.

O day dawn, O strange dawn,
    And is it true what they say,
That you'll come at last to the sweet, sweet dead,
    And will you to mine some day?

WHO PLANTS A TREE.

Who plants a tree, he is akin to God.
    In this impatient age
    Where quick rewards engage
  The fevered service of the crowd,
  In reverent wisdom he is bowed
And hides his distant purpose in the clod.

The blessed man that plants a long-lived tree
    That shall grow nobly on
    When he is dead and gone,
  He seems to me to love his kind
  With true sincerity of mind;
He seems to love his fellows yet to be.

Above his grave the suns shall flush and fade,
    The seasons come and go,
    And storms shall drive and blow;
  But sun and rain, that from his tomb
  Efface his name, renew the bloom
And glory of this monument he made.

Perhaps our God somewhere has made a thing
    More admirable to see
    Than a majestic tree;
  But if He has, I think it grows
  In Heaven, by the stream that flows
Along where whiter souls than ours sing.

THE SACRAMENT OF SPRING.

"I went down into the garden of nuts to see the fruits of the valley, and to see whether the vine flourished, and the pomegranates budded. Or ever I was aware, my soul made me like the chariots of Ammi-nadib!"—Song of Solomon vi. 11-12.

As when the young priest first comes close
To altar lights and reredos,
And lifts his hand to take the cup
Wherein God's blood is gathered up,
So stand I hushed and wondering
Before the Epiphany of Spring.
A light incipient ecstacy
Of earth and air encircles me;
A tender glory, ill-concealed;
A strange, new story, half-revealed;
A vague, prophetic incompleteness;
A heart of heart's bemusing sweetness.

I know the Summer cannot pay
The lavish promise of today;
I know that when the story's told
Soon will it irk us and grow old;
I know, I know— but hearts flame out
And burn the barriers of doubt.
For Oh! what swelling joy to stand
Just on the smiling borderland
Where Spring and Youth and Love unfold
And throw their mists of fairy gold
O'er all the doubting world! Arise,
Sad heart, believe this day's surprise;
And join the season's Passion-play
Of Miracle and Mystery!

Help, Lord, the sodden unbelief
　Of Winter's lingering leaf
　　And moldering sheaf
　　　Of grief!

The choiring bees begin to sing,
The mitred buds appear and fling
Their incense round us, worshipping
At Nature's shrine.　In everything
God's still, small voice is whispering.
This is the Sacrament of Spring!

"I AM."

"Before Abraham was, I am."

The little Christ that lay on Mary's breast,
The babe the medieval mind caressed,
   Is not my Jesus; mine's a new-born hope
That builds each morn within my life its nest.

The Christ that once in ancient Galilee
Strewed golden parables beside the sea,
   Is not my Lord: He vaster walks to-day
The avenues of souls and talks with me.

That Christ between two thieves there on the hill
Is not the Son of God we helped to kill;
   In slum and prison, nailed twixt law and lust,
Hangs the dim Horror of our common will.

Behold, behold Him, all ye that pass by,
The Christ! And hear His low, perpetual cry,
   From ashen lips the moan of hearts abandoned,
"Eli, Eli, lama sabachthani!"

There was no Christ, I say! That thorn-set brow
Was not, but is, eternally is now!
   Up through the hate of centuries, He bears
The unwilling world to peace, we know not how.

LIVE LIKE A FLOWER.

A Song.

  Live like a flower, my love,
   Live like a flower!
Look on the lily in the garden growing,
So timid-frail, yet with bold beauty glowing.
  Live like a flower, my love,
   Live like a flower!

It must please God to see how brave she lifts
Her white, sweet hands to take His royal gifts.
  Live like a flower, my love,
   Live like a flower!

She has no thorn to bruise her trustful breast,
No fear that life and sunshine be not best.
  Live like a flower, my love,
   Live like a flower!

And thou, when these dear human joys will come
To thy heart's door, why, bid them welcome—home!
  Live like a flower, my love,
   Live like a flower!

Alas! why think we so divine the rod,
But dare not trust that pleasure comes from God?
  Live like a flower, my love,
   Live like a flower!

Take sorrow—this we must: and so I say,
Take sweets and heart's-ease, too—for this we may.
  Live like a flower, my love,
   Live like a flower!

EASTER GREETING.

Give me a heart for Easter,
        A bold heart,
        Not an old heart,
Heart of six or heart of ten,
  Or sixty and ten young again,
That's the heart for Easter!

Give me a smile for Easter,
        A glad smile,
        Not a sad smile,
A smile that lies on lips and eyes,
  A ripple of inward harmonies,
That's the smile for Easter!

Give me a word for Easter,
        A cheery word,
        Not a teary word,
A word that's like the break o' day,
  That scatters the bats and blues away,
That's the word for Easter.

SHEPHERD'S REST.

"And when He had sent the multitude away, He went up into a mountain apart to pray: and when evening was come He was there alone.

"But the ship, in which were His disciples, was now in the midst of the sea, tossed with waves; for the wind was contrary."

"And in the fourth watch of the night Jesus went unto them, walking on the sea."   St. Matthew xiv: 23-25.

    Alone on the solemn mountain,
        Where walks the ghost of day,
    The Master has fled to the silence,
        And gone apart to pray.

    Where deep in the whispering stillness
        Stand sentinel the trees,
    Is a shadow within the shadow,
        A moaning within the breeze.

    It is O for a moment of breathing,
        In the stress of the cruel race!
    And it's O to reach up in the darkness
        And feel the Father's face!

    But hark! far down in the valley
        Is the bleating of sheep distressed.
    Rise up, O shepherd-hearted!
        What has Love to do with Rest?

THE LITTLE WHITE BIRCHES OF NEW ENGLAND.

Have you ever seen
The little white birches of New England?
First of all the wood people
They catch the eye of the lover.

Scattered through the dun forest,
In autumn, white against dark trunks,
Smooth against elm, oak and hickory,
The birches appear like maidens,
White robed, supple and slender,
Going out to welcome an army,
Mingling among mailed warriors,
Returning victorious from summer.

Where they gather in clusters,
It is as if tall dryads
Had fled to the fern-covered hill-side,
Or rebellious had trooped to the lowland,
And there had been metamorphosed
Into slim trees, swaying,
Plotting and whispering forever.

Have you seen they never grow upright,
But always as if springing sidewise?
"Escape! escape!" says their gesture,
Sweeping with swift grace skyward,
From the brown grass to the white clouds;
Or ever you are aware,
Your heart has fluttered and flown with them.

What are they? Are they the bare arms,
The long, rounded, girlish bare arms
Of some buried new-world Krishna,

Ashtoreth, Venus or Isis,
Dead grace of forgotten ages,
Waving, urging still upward
All questioning souls that pass by?

Or are they but thin wraiths, sinuous
Spectres of ancestral tree-nobles?

Sometimes as I round the hill's shoulder
And spy them among the green pines,
Picked out sharp on the dark green,
They come over my soul
Like sharp articulate cries.

In summer, I remember,
Glimpsed through diaphanous leafage,
Their nude beauty startled and charmed me,
As the nymphs of Diana's chorus,
At play in their bosky seclusion,
Might have ravished the eye profane
Of some wandering peasant of Hellas,
Lost in the heather of Hymettus,
In the days when all living things had souls.

O little white birches of New England,
You have caught my heart in your branches!
All night like questing star-sisters
You march through my dreams processional,
Weirdly beckoning, calling up
Nameless ivory fancies.

O my little sisters,
He who has never seen you
Has never seen trees praying.

—Worcester, Mass.

THREE THINGS.

Three things are terrible to meet:
  A ship abandoned on the seas,
  A ruined house among the trees,
And a lost soul in the city street.
—*London.*

THE LOST DREAM.

Through the wealth of the Spring-time wandered a soul weeping;
She seemed upon some fearful quest.
She searched among the cherry-blossoms,
She looked long into the cup of the lily,
She sought among the violets, turning back the broad leaves, and peering anxiously under the blue flowers,
She ranged the great sky, sorting and dividing the colors of the sunset, and examining the flocking clouds as they hastened by,
And went inquiring of the brooks,
And watched the uncoiling of the fern-leaves,
And noted the songs of the birds,
And at last sat down upon the sand
Where the sea sobs forever,
And wept, as the sea weeps.
—What seekest thou, O soul?
And what rare thing has thou lost?
—I have lost my dream!

BALLAD OF THE DEAD.

Through all my journey long, between
  The two eternities,
A woman ever dogged my steps
  With importunities.

I never saw her face, but Oh
  When she would darkly creep
Close to me in her muffled robe
  My heart would writhe and weep.

At last I neared my narrow house—
  It lay just on before—
But when I reached the gate, there stood
  That woman at the door.

"What is thy name?" I cried dismayed.
  "What dost thou in this place?"
"Sorrow!" she answered, and let fall
  Her robe, I saw her face.

So sweet it was, my heart stood still
  And never beat again:
Sweet with God's sweetness, so my breath
  Went out in happy pain.

"Ah! sweet, my love!" I murmured, "Stay
  With me all heaven's years!
My heart is dry and thirsts for aye
  To blossom in thy tears."

She smiled—'twas like Christ's smile—and said,
  "Both thou and I must cease:
But—take my soul to cheer thy soul,
  For Sorrow's soul is Peace."

MY FRIEND.

He is my friend who loves me true,
    Whate'er I do;
Who loves me, and yet more than me,
    What I might be;
Whose trust in me's not even stirred
    By my own word;
Who's loyal to me even when I
    Myself belie.
I think, with such a friend, I'd be
    Even such as he.

WHEN SHE COMES HOME.

How will the air
    Color and sweeten
And all the world grow young;
    This house we meet in
    And everywhere
With prism lights be flung—
        When she comes home!

How will her eye
    Drench my dry heart
With one o'er-brimmed glance!
    How, with a start,
    Will passion cry
And young desires dance—
        When she comes home!

I'll touch her hand—
    Her hand at first—
Only her hand so dear,
    My cruel thirst
    I will command
When love's full cup is here—
        When she comes home!

I'll kiss her brow,
    Her odorous hair,
Her eyelids—ere her lips.
    I must beware
    Lest from me now,
(As in those dreams,) she slips—
        When she comes home!

When she comes home—
    My love! my life!—
Comes heaven in her train,
    My sweet! my wife!
Heart's-ease will come—
And breath of life again—
    When she comes home!

—Chicago.

CHRISTMAS WISHES.

O may the little babies all,
    Upon this Christmas night,
In hovel or in castle hall,
    Be dimpled with delight;
And may they gently, gently sleep,
    Or wake to sweetly smile;
And may the tender Jesus keep
    His watch o'er them the while!

May all the little girls and boys
    Beneath the heaven's blue
Have all imaginable toys
    And love and laughter too!
God grant, while it is thus so cheap
    To fill their lives with light,
That never one be made to weep
    Upon this Christmas night!

Young men and maids, where'er ye be,
    Put on your gay attire,
And may true love and guileless glee
    Be all your heart's desire!
May all the sweets ye revel in
    Be those that never cloy;
And may no shadow of a sin,
    Lie dark across your joy!

May all stern men and cruel men
    Feel some strange gentleness,
May sad men and despairing men
    To-night feel hope's caress.
May every mother in the world
    Hear good news of her child,
And every weary heart be furled
    In Christ's heart meek and mild!

And O, upon the silver head
    Of age may heaven's light,
Like sunset's last bright beams, be shed
    In holy peace to-night!
May hate and greed, and all that's wrong,
    Be shamed and smitten, when
The choiring angels sing their song
    Of "Peace, good will to men!"

THE GATES OF HEAVEN.

Three broad bars of blush
Spring from the dead sun's golden after-glow
And fan-like spread the western sky;
Between them lies the deep blue firmament,
Blue, blue, so blue I almost touch its rich intensity;
Across the sky lies a single, lancinate, long cloud,
Mottled and flocculent,
Dying away dappling in the distance;
Up to the south a little hangs a star,
The star of stars,
Venus!
Ah, when those Greeks,
Finding in visible beauty the only fit answer
To the rising sweetness of young passion,
Saw thee, thou lambent, trembling drop,
Gracing the reddening breast of youthful even,
Like a diamond upon the warm neck of a girl,
I do not wonder that they called thee—Love!

Is heaven like this?
This answer of the soul to God's beauty,
This rushing back of all forgotten joys,
This quick bounding into birth of a myriad rare conceits,
All these—is Heaven like this?

—*At Sea.*

THE LONELIEST SPOT.

Is there a silence more profound
Than o'er the grass-grown battle-ground,
Or place where stiller shadows cower
Than in the ruined castle's tower,
Or sharper solitude than falls
In late deserted banquet-halls,
Or in the hollow church, when prayer
And song and souls have vanished there?
Is there a sight more woe-begone
Than London streets before the dawn,
Or ghastlier spot by night or day
Than the painted walls of old Pompeii?

Yes, there's a lonelier, darker spot,
The heart where love was—and is not!
—*Heidelberg.*

THE ANSWER.

"Now curses upon thee, Book!
And curse thy tyranny!
And cursed be thy laws," he said
"That lie so hard on me!"

Then the leaves of the Book were moved
And they answered the challenge of dust;
"He shall cover thee with His feathers,
And under His wings shalt thou trust!"
—*Bloomington.*

TRUTH.

Woe! woe! for I have seen the dark side of truth!
        Not clear and bright
        With eternal light,
    But cruel and black and full of wrath,
    With the lurid look that perdition hath,
        Without mercy or ruth—
Woe unto me that I've seen the dark side of truth!

Truth is a double thing to all the sons of men:
        To them that hear
        And obey in fear
    She opens the secrets of ultimate peace;
    But her pitiless vengence doth ever increase
        'Gainst the foolish, when
They flee from the high word she gives to the sons of men.

Truth never whispers of heaven without an echo of hell;
        The same sun and air
        That ripen the pear
    Will rot it and blight it when life is gone.
    The agents of health and disease are one
        To sick and to well;
Truth leads the obedient to heaven and lashes the coward to hell.

MORNING ON LAKE MICHIGAN.

The lake this morning 's like a girl's blue eye,
Hazy with reverie, and strange, dim hopes.
Blue, touched with green, it lies spread peacefully
Far from my feet unto the misty distance,
Becoming paler still as it recedes
And slips at last into the whiter sky;
The heaven and the water married there
In that invisible horizon, hid
Behind a nuptial veil of lustrous gauze.

The sunlight falls not sharp and brilliant now,
But seems as if suffusing all the air—
It is not light, but light's soft shining ghost.

Across the blue-green water steal the shadows,
Blotches of purple shade from wandering clouds,
As tranquil thoughts glide o'er a happy mind.

The lake this morning 's like a girl's blue eye;
And as I look at its wide mystery,
It is as if I saw a vast, still soul,
Sweet as a dawning love, serene as God.
—*Chicago Beach Hotel.*

WHY I LOVE YOU.

I've sometimes thought it was your eyes,
    Sometimes your voice,
Bade my indifferent heart arise
    And make its choice.

I've counted over all your ways,
    My sweet, my mate,
And wondered which the separate grace
    That held my fate.

Vain task! I love you, dearest one,
    For all you are—
The charm of heaven hangs not upon
    A single star.
—Island Grove.

THE LITTLE GREEN SNAKE.

O there was a young man,
And he found a little green snake,
    A neat snake,
    A sweet snake,
And after her he ran,
A gaily crested, purple vested green snake.

O she lay upon his breast,
Did this coiling little little green snake,
    This lisping snake,
    And whispering snake,
In his heart she made her nest,
Did this blushing little, flushing little green snake.

O he pressed her to his side,
This so dear a little green snake,
    This pure snake,
    And demure snake,
And she stung him that he died,
This playful, twining, gay and shining green snake.

THE UNCHOSEN CROSS.

    I do not know. He knows. But I know Him!

Why am I chosen for nobility?
Why am I put where I for very shame
Must play the hero? I, who only wish
To sing my songs beside some peaceful stream,
And idly pluck the tranquil flowers of life?
Ah me! and I am thrust into the stress of pain,
And I must dare and suffer and be great;
Like Simon of Cyrene, who craned his neck
Among the curious to see the Christ,
And was impressed by ribald soldiery
To bear the Cross he neither sought nor knew!
Why? why? I ask, a querulous, fretful why!
I may not know, but this alone I know;
The Cross is laid on all, on man, God, too,
And even on devils. Shall I bear it then
Like devils, sunk by it, drowned in despair,
Or shall I, like the calm and patient Christ,
Bear it to death, that it bear me to peace?

    I do not know. He knows. But I know Him!

A PRAYER.

O Christ, I know not what
    Of joy or sorrow,
My next day hath for me—
    Here, take Tomorrow!

Shall I not be afraid,
    When, at the last,
I face the Judgment Bar?
    Here, take my Past!

How shall I ever reach
    The Blessed Land,
Unless thou guide me still?
    Here, take my Hand!

My fitful passions draw
    My soul apart
Ever from thy dear ways—
    Here, take my Heart!

For all thy care for me,
    So manifold,
What can I render thee?
    Here, take my Gold!

Life is too hard, dear Lord,
    I only fall
When I would bear its load—
    Here, take my All.
               —*Union Church.*

THE LOST WORD.

"While I was musing the fire burned;"
I knew not what it was,
Whether a great thought, a feeling, an idea;
I only know that my soul was like to break
With its power, its strange truth, its overmastering sweetness.
I sought a WORD to express it,
Lest I die of it.
So I read the inspired prophets,
Poets, lovers, mystics, dreamers;
I listened to the music of the masters,
And stood long before great paintings;
I studied orators, actors, preachers,
Who deal in words,
But their words touched not upon my WORD;
I sent my soul into life's tragic hours,
Among mad men at the battle's core,
Among revelers in debauch,
By the bedside of the dying;
I listened to the prayers of saints,
And to the epithalamia of lovers;
Yet I found not the WORD I sought.
Then, one night, I awoke—
And to me came my soul's bride,
Clothed in unflecked darkness,
And at last I had found my WORD,
The flawless bride of thought,
She whose presence alone answers to the deepest feeling;
Her name is—SILENCE!

INVITATION TO VESPERS.

Come, O my friend, awhile with me,
What time the crystal of the sky
Is thickening in the violet east;
When, flaming through the west, we see
The sun's last crimson sigh. O come,
And in the solemn, stately Church,
Still your uneasy life! Your eye
Will clear to see the invisible,
Your ear to hear the still, small voice.
Hark! hear those sounds fly, velvet-winged,
Among the arches, fluttering
Like blessed ghosts unprisoned from
The sweet great-organ's clustered pipes!
Does not each cadence sooth and cool
The fever of some morbid care?
Pray, friend! You'll find our common prayer
Shall teach your laboring soul to fly.
Come, sing! the hymn dissolves the doubt.
Look! as the sunlight dims, the nave
Is fretted all with glowing lamps!
So shall we be transfigured, too;
And our crass, glaring worldliness
Change to the inner light of God.
—*Union Church.*

THE WATERS OF BETHLEHEM.

"And David longed, and said, 'Oh that one would give me drink of the water of the well of Bethlehem, that is at the gate!'" I Chronicles xi: 17.

 O fallen in life's desert lands,
  O traveller by mistaken ways,
 Behold, above the heated sands
  The sweet mirage of earlier days!

 Ah memory, dip thy finger tip
  In some cool well of distant youth,
 And touch the doubter's drying lip,
  With but one drop of living truth!

THE THREE AGES.

A child one day, in the twilight gray,
    Sat wishing he were a man,
His little thought with fancies fraught
    Through all the wide years ran.

A man passed by, and with a sigh
    Wished that he were a boy,
Though he wore the crown of great renown
    His heart it wore no joy.

And last there came an old man lame,
    Hanging his hoary head,
Not older wished he nor younger to be
    But only that he were dead.

RAIN ON THE LAKE.

I wonder why it rains
    Upon the lake?
Heaven must have more for earth
    Than earth can take.

Life overcrowds the world,
    The insistent seed
Swarms o'er the roadside, where
    There is no need.

Heart of dead hope, around
    Thy hungry grave
Rich fields of unreaped faith
    Beckon and wave.

And those vast steppes of death,
    To us so still,
With myriad vibrant lives
    Echo and thrill.
        —*Chicago Beach Hotel.*

A FIGURE8IVE TALE.

8ender tale I now rel8
In figure8tive speech.
                    As f8
Gives me no power to corrusc8
In metaphor and trope orn8,
I'll use my lowlier gifts, and st8
My facts in humble figure—8.

Young, beautiful and lissome K8
Was loved and wooed by William W8,
Daily, as they together s8,
And nightly, at the garden g8;
Yet when he'd ask her if she'd m8
She ever answered, "William, w8!"

He'd show her all his love so gr8,
He'd argue every night till 18,
And would at length expati8
Upon his cheerless, lonely f8.
He'd plead with her to fix the d8,
But she would not particip8
In his long, amorous deb8,
But would her forehead corrug8
And coyly answer: "William, w8!"

"At least," he cried, "O maid sed8,
Though it my woe may aggrav8,
Tell, O I pray thee, tell me str8,
Hast thou a lover? O rel8
His h8ful name, and seal my f8!"
She blushing murmured: "William, w8!"

"I see" he did ejacul8,
" 'Tis I! 'Tis I! I'm William W8!"
He clasps the maiden rose8,
Their hearts in rapturous bliss puls8.
"And may I kiss thee once, dear K8?
Just one sweet kiss? Say yes! O s8!"
Demure she whispered: "7 or 8."
They kissed. 'Twas March of '88.
By June they'd scored 8,000,008.

SEQUEL.

They're married now, and, sad to st8,
When she asks for a kiss, the gr8
Big brute does thus retali8:
"W8, K8; w8, Mrs. K8 W8, w8!"

—*Omaha.*

SECRET WOE.

Now God be nigh his wordless cry
    Who may not his sorrows tell!
For he stands on the edge of the crumbling ledge
    That borders the deeps of hell!

THE TEMPLE OF UNBELIEF.

I went to the Church of the Agnostic,
The Temple of Unbelief.
I saw there an altar without lights,
The priest was blind and dumb,
Dust was in the cup, and dried blood,
And the people—their lips smiled, while their hearts wept.
There was sorrow, not for sin,
But for sin's price.
They prayed, not for forgiveness
But for forgetfulness,
And the feeling that drew them there
Was not eternal love
But eternal longing.

—*Paris.*

DESPAIR.

O Gesù, Gesù, make my bed,
    And tenderly tuck the sod,
Draw the green-grass coverlet over my head
    And forget to tell my God!

"THERE IS A DIMPLE."

"Good friend, for Jesus' sake forbear
To dig the dust that's buried here;
Blest be the man that spares these stones,
And curst be he that moves my bones!"
—*Epitaph on Shakespeare's Tomb.*

There is a dimple on one side your mouth,
(Comes scorn from such a jasmine-fragrant mouth?)
Where I lie buried, where my soul lies hid—
(O, veil your deadly eye with half-dropped lid!)
    Your eye looked out and laughed,
    Poison with sly witchcraft;
      I caught the barbed dart
      Full in my heart—
      Then did all sense depart,
        Hearing, Seeing,
        Even Being,
          All but a tremulous breath
            Of Feeling—that is surely Death!
          You held my soul beneath
          Full lip and flashing teeth
        And shrivelled it in the fire
        Of masterless desire
      Till it was cinder—
      How could I hinder?
    You blew the ashen spirit then away:
    It fell and lay
    Dead in your dimple—lies there still to-day,
    Waiting until your penitent lips shall say:
    "I love you." What a resurrection day!
No other wakening for such death atones,
Dare not with other words to move my bones!

"THIS, TOO, SHALL PASS."

Night and day, night and day!
Thus my life is told away
By the alternating shift of light and shade;
For to-day I sit and brood,
And but yesterday my mood
Was as gay as merry music ever played.

So I comfort me with this,
When my soul in sorrow is,
That the day is slowly, slowly creeping up;
And when I am drinking joy
I 'll remember, lest it cloy,
Tears are always in the bottom of the cup.

GOODBYE!

Goodbye! goodbye! I 'll say goodbye
    Between these trembling kisses:
The parting breath of dreaded Death
    Is not so sad as this is!

Goodbye! goodbye! One broken cry!
    And thou art mine no longer!
Though sweet and strong Love's silken thong,
    The chain of Fate is stronger.

Goodbye, O Flower! A little hour
    I saw thee bloom before me:
But through the tears of lonely years
    Thy fragrance shall be o'er me!

SACRED HEART.

O Sacred Heart, how filled
    With all the troops of woe!
O Loyal Heart, that willed
    For us to open so!
And where the spear-point burst the door
    The suffering enter evermore,
    Their peace to gain
    Through gates of pain.

O Sacred Heart, how stilled
    Beneath the cruel blow!
O Sacred Blood, how spilled
    Upon the ground below!
And earth has never been the same
    Since on its breast that dark spot came;
    It feels Thy blood,
    O Son of God!

THE CHRIST CHILD.

O holy Child! to Thee
Do architect and artist plan
The proudest, grandest works of man,
Dreams wrought in masonry.

O holy Child! to Thee
Poets their lyric diadems
Of beauty bring, all set with gems
Of tender fantasy.

O holy Child! to show
Us how the seraphs 'round Thee ring
Genius hath soared on stately wing
In oratorio.

O holy Child! my part
May never be such tribute rare,
But on my sinful knees in prayer
I bring Thee all my heart!

Invention is held in check by Providence to wait on social evolution; Providence will not suffer this age, with its false economics, to discover aerial locomotion or the secret of telepathy.

Few rich men are worthy of riches; but for that matter few poor men appreciate or deserve the privileges of poverty.

The gist of religion was in the remark the dying Bunsen made to his wife, as she stooped over him: "In thy face have I seen the Eternal."

In the heart of yielding there is happiness; but in the heart of self-denial there is joy.

Perfect faith is courteous; intolerance is a sign of a subtle disbelief in the power of truth.

Accuracy is far from being truth. What is true is often vague.

The Christ of the first centuries was a miracle worker; the Christ of the twentieth century is permanent, recognized power.

Nothing is absolutely true unless it can be set to music.

The most improbable thing one knows is one's own life.

Opinion is a guest at the inn: belief is the master of the house.

The truest knowing-power is love; we only know through and through what we love.

One of the most difficult things is to appreciate a gift, and to know how to render its spiritual equivalent.

Every soul is surrounded by a sort of penumbra, wherein lies the most of its sin and holiness.

Wishes are the odors of the heart. By them you may know whether, at the core of you, you are a rose or a cesspool.

Economize everywhere but in love. There the law of life is prodigality, waste, reckless profusion.

What any man does, whether in art, or business, or religion, is but a faint echo of what the universe has done to him.

The cohesive element in parties and sects is not unity of opinion, but community of ignorance. It is not what we know that makes us hang together, but what we do not know.

By these marks we can know that God has touched the heart: when a little thought gives way to a large thought; when willingness to use a lie is replaced by a loyalty to truth; when fear is changed to courage; when conscientiousness begins to extend also into the dark; when anger is mastered by self-control; when peevishness becomes sweetness; when jealousy and envy are transformed into real happiness in another's welfare; when we find pleasure in duty; when love of ease disappears before a desire to satisfy our sense of ought; and when flippancy, as a habit of mind, is replaced by reverence.

I ask not what quality has been the river of your days, but what has been its sediment upon your heart.

It was not only because Jesus gave us ideas, revelations and spiritual insight, but also, as well, because He received food, shelter and human sympathy, that He links us to the infinite. We worship the God who gives, we love the God who takes.

Words—we utter them lightly, yet each one of them is the coral remnant of vanished souls: these souls lived, strived, worked, they went away then, leaving us only this shell they had secreted—a word.

The devil is called "the prince of this world" in the Bible; and it is as true now as it was in Judea that the way to go to the devil is to do as others do.

Most men looking back can trace their spiritual downfall to the time when they chose success and subscribed to the creed: "Ideals are unsafe."

The opposite of reverence is vulgarity; an irreverent person is vulgar in the heart of him.

To have a right to doubt requires as blameless a rectitude of life as does the right to call one's self a Christian. Neither your doubt or your faith is entitled to any respect unless backed up by character.

The gospel is not addressed to a man, but to what a man knows he might be.

The works of the imagination are more stable than facts so-called. Who knows anything about the kings and rich men of Homer's day? So the nabobs of ancient India lie pulverized in oblivion, while we tell the folk-story of the Hindu hut still to our children. Queen Elizabeth is remembered as the contemporary of Shakespeare, and Napoleon as one who lived in Goethe's day.

There is no such thing as sin, just as there is no such thing as cold; cold is the absence of heat, and sin is the absence of control over the forces from within us.

To put heart into one's work it is better to believe than to know: the man of faith works heartier than a man of experience.

The imagination has far more to do with a child's future happiness than his reason or memory, and yet in our systems of education its culture is practically neglected.

Faith has its illusions; unbelief its delusions.

Life is the most complex of all things, and therefore the ultimate virtue is the power of adjustment.

Most of the things that enrich life overtake us as we flee from them.

Of all creeds the worst is the coward's creed, that suffering is the chief thing to be avoided.

WS - #0198 - 100225 - C0 - 229/152/3 - PB - 9781331230045 - Gloss Lamination